Gulp and Gasp

The Spirals Series

Fiction

Jim Alderson
The Witch Princess

Penny Bates
Tiger of the Lake

Jan Carew
Footprints in the Sand
Voices in the Dark

Susan Duberley
The Ring

John Goodwin
Ghost Train

Angela Griffiths
Diary of a Wild Thing
Stories of Suspense

Anita Jackson
The Actor
The Austin Seven
Bennet Manor
Dreams
The Ear
A Game of Life and Death
No Rent to Pay

Paul Jennings
Maggot

Richard Kemble
Grandmother's Secret

Helen Lowerson
The Biz

Margaret Loxton
The Dark Shadow

Bill Ridgway
The Hawkstone
Mr Punch

John Townsend
Back on the Prowl
A Minute to Kill
Night Beast
Snow Beast

Plays

Jan Carew
Computer Killer

Chris Culshaw
Radio Riff-Raff

Julia Donaldson
Books and Crooks

Angela Griffiths
TV Hospital
Wally and Co.

Paul Groves
Tell Me Where it Hurts

Bill Ridgway
Monkey Business

John Townsend
A Bit of a Shambles
Books and Crooks
Clogging the Works
Cowboys, Jelly and Custard
Hiccups and Slip-ups
Jumping the Gun
A Lot of Old Codswallop
Murder at Muckleby Manor

David Walke
The Good, the Bad and the Bungle
Package Holiday

Non-fiction

Jim Alderson
Crash in the Jungle

Chris Culshaw
Dive into Danger

David Orme
Hackers

Jill Ridge
Lifelines

Bill Ridgway
Lost in Alaska
Over the Wall

Julie Taylor
Lucky Dip

John Townsend
Burke and Hare: The Body Snatchers
Kingdom of the Man-eaters

PLAYS

Gulp and Gasp

John Townsend

Text © John Townsend 2002

The right of John Townsend to be identified as author of this work has been asserted by him in accordance with the Copyright, Designs and Patents Act 1988.

All rights reserved. No part of this publication may be reproduced or transmitted in any form or by any means, electronic or mechanical, including photocopy, recording or any information storage and retrieval system, without permission in writing from the publisher or under licence from the Copyright Licensing Agency Limited, of Saffron House, 6–10 Kirby Street, London EC1N 8TS.

Any person who commits any unauthorised act in relation to this publication may be liable to criminal prosecution and civil claims for damages.

Published in 2002 by:
Nelson Thornes Ltd
Delta Place
27 Bath Road
CHELTENHAM
GL53 7TH
United Kingdom

07 08 09 10 / 10 9 8 7 6 5 4 3 2

A catalogue record for this book is available from the British Library

ISBN 978 0 7487 6681 9

Cover illustration by Harry Venning
Page make-up by Tech-Set, Gateshead

Printed in Croatia by Zrinski

Gulp and Gasp

A shocking old-time drama of villains, a damsel and a dashing hero. A play for four parts.

Cast in order of appearance

Lord Septic The nasty boss of the railways. A cruel and evil villain of the worst sort.

Crouch His slimy little servant – a bully who grovels for a living.

Rose A pure, young and pretty damsel in distress.

Percy The dashing hero – handsome, brave and squeaky clean . . . right down to his undies.

Scene: An empty railway station at night. It is cold and foggy. Lord Septic stomps up and down the platform under a gas lamp. Crouch carries his bags, running along behind him.

Lord Septic	It's late.
Crouch	Mmm.
Lord Septic	Very late.
Crouch	Mmm. Mmm.
Lord Septic	My train is late.
Crouch	Indeed, sir.
Lord Septic	Foul.
Crouch	Mmm.
Lord Septic	Horrid.
Crouch	Indeed, sir.
Lord Septic	Filthy . . .
Crouch	Really? [*He looks at his shoes*] Did you tread in something, sir?
Lord Septic	The night, you fool. It's a foul and filthy night.
Crouch	Very nasty, Lord Septic.
Lord Septic	Angry.
Crouch	Mmm.
Lord Septic	Very angry.
Crouch	Mmm. Mmmm.

Lord Septic	And do you know why I'm angry, Crouch? I hate nights like this.
Crouch	Indeed, sir.
Lord Septic	This fog is so thick. I can't see a thing out there. It's as thick as . . .
Crouch	Pea soup, sir. Very thick pea soup.
Lord Septic	And there's nothing worse than pea soup is there, Crouch?
Crouch	Not really, sir. Apart from sprouts. I would think a mushy sprout soup is pretty foul. Worse than a pea in this fog.
Lord Septic	I can't even see the railway track.
Crouch	Don't get too near the edge of the platform, sir.
Lord Septic	If this train doesn't come soon, I'll sack the driver. I'll sack everyone. After all, next week I'll own this railway line.
Crouch	Indeed, sir. Most true, your ever-so big lordship, sir.
Lord Septic	Nothing can stop me now. I'm just a step away. Do you know what I'm just a step away from?
Crouch	Yes. The edge of the platform. Be careful, sir.
Lord Septic	No, you fool! Power. Money. Fame.
Crouch	But you've got quite of bit of that already.

Lord Septic	More! I want more, Crouch. I need it. I long for it. I'm mad for it. I'll kill for it.
Crouch	And you always want what you get, sir.
Lord Septic	No, Crouch. I always get what I want. At last, I own this station. Soon I will own all the stations from here to King's Cross. And when I do . . . do you know what I'll be?
Crouch	Even more greedy, sir?
Lord Septic	I'll be the richest man in the land. And do you know why?
Crouch	Because you'll own the biggest train set ever.
Lord Septic	Because I will find the Gatsby Gold. It's hidden somewhere along this line. I'll dig up the track. I'll look under every sleeper. I'll search every station. One day, it will be mine. All mine. At last . . . And nothing will get in my way. [*He trips over Crouch*] Get out of my way, you fool.
Crouch	Most sorry, sir. Very sorry, sir. Really sorry, sir.
Lord Septic	I'll now go up to my office to plot more plans. I'll get more ideas on being rich. Filthy rich. Thick, black and oily. That's how rich! I'm going upstairs.
Crouch	Don't get too many ideas above your station, sir!

Lord Septic	Shut up, you half-wit. Just stay here and tell me when the train comes. You know what tonight is, don't you?
Crouch	Oh yes, sir. It's cold, sir.
Lord Septic	Try the letter 'F', Crouch.
Crouch	The letter 'F', sir?
Lord Septic	Tonight is an 'F' night.
Crouch	Er . . . frosty?
Lord Septic	Try again.
Crouch	Foggy? It's a very foggy night, sir.
Lord Septic	I'm getting more angry, Crouch.
Crouch	I'm not very good with letters, sir.
Lord Septic	'F', Crouch. Tonight is an 'F'. Got it?
Crouch	Yes, sir. It's a freezing, filthy, frosty, foggy, foul night. That's a lot of 'F's.
Lord Septic	It's a FRIDAY night, Crouch. And you know what that means.
Crouch	Indeed your lordship. Of course, sir. Indeed I do. It means . . . tomorrow is Saturday.
Lord Septic	It means it's the end of the week. It means I need to get back to my country castle. I have a hunting party this weekend. I need to kill.
Crouch	Oh, really, sir?

Lord Septic My wife will be waiting.

Crouch You need to kill your wife, sir?

Lord Septic Don't be a dim-wit, Crouch. Mind you, it wouldn't be a bad idea! Clora is a pain in the neck.

Crouch Clora?

Lord Septic Yes, Clora – my wife. Clora Septic. She nags for a living. I only married her for her arms.

Crouch Are they nice to hug?

Lord Septic Not those arms. She owns a gun factory. We make weapons. We make bombs. One day we will arm the world. We want a good war. She's just made a tank that can kill from a mile in one burst. Just like her! It's called the Septic Tank.

Crouch I bet that'll cause a bit of a stink, sir!

Lord Septic Crouch, I don't know why I keep you as my porter. You are dim, daft, dopey, dozey and dippy. What's more, you annoy me. I'm not nice when I'm cross.

Crouch No, sir.

Lord Septic And now I'm tired, cold and fed up.

Crouch That's another 'F' word, sir.

Lord Septic	And to make it worse . . . I think I just saw another 'F' under the clock.

[*Rose enters, looking like a ghost*]

Crouch	A f . . . f . . . f . . . phantom, sir?
Lord Septic	A flower seller. I will not have beggars on my platform. Tell her to go or I'll throw her and her flowers under the midnight express – if it ever comes.
Crouch	Leave it to me, sir.
Lord Septic	Call me when the train comes. [*He leaves*]
Crouch	Very well, sir. Now then, I shall enjoy this. At last I have some power . . . Oi!
Rose	Hello?
Crouch	What do you think you're doing?
Rose	Would you like a few lovely flowers, sir? Only a penny a bunch.
Crouch	Shut up. Clear off. Get lost.
Rose	I'll take that as a no, then.
Crouch	Get off this platform. We don't have beggars here.
Rose	But I'm just a poor harmless flower seller.
Crouch	Then you shouldn't be out on a night like this. On such a dark and foggy night you could get lost . . . ha ha ha.

Rose	It's the same to me if it's night or day.
Crouch	What do you mean, you fool?
Rose	I'm blind.
Crouch	Blind?
Rose	Yes, sir. Do buy a sprig of heather for a penny. It may bring you good luck.
Crouch	I told you: NO BEGGARS. If Lord Septic sees you, he'll throw you on to the track . . . lucky heather and all . . . ha ha ha.
Rose	Lord Septic? Not THE Lord Septic?
Crouch	Yes, his lordship. The man who runs this town. The man who will soon own all the trains. The man who will soon be mayor.
Rose	The man who's wrecked my life.
Crouch	The man who told you to GET OFF THIS PLATFORM!
Rose	But I can't go home till I earn a few coins. My mother is so sick and I must pay for the pills that will make her well. I haven't eaten for three days.
Crouch	Who cares?
Rose	If I can just sell a few flowers I may be able to pay the doctors. I'm trying to save up for an operation on my eyes. Then I will be able to see again.

Crouch	Bah! Who cares about that? It doesn't matter if you can see or not on a night like this.
Rose	Please . . . I beg you.
Crouch	We don't have beggars here. Now get out of here and keep this platform free of filth . . . of vermin . . . of scum. [*He throws her tray of flowers across the platform*]
[*HISS*]	
Rose	But these flowers are all I have.
Crouch	Unlucky. It looks like your lucky heather ain't so lucky after all! Ha ha ha. I'm going to tell Lord Septic I've sent you on your way. But I warn you, if you haven't gone by the time I come back, you and your flowers will be pulp under the next train. [*He leaves*]
[*BOO*]	
Rose	[*She sobs as she tries to find her flowers*] What can I do? Where can I go? It's so cold. I can't feel my fingers. I can't find my flowers. If only I could see. If only I had a few coins. I can't go home without money. We'll starve. Poor mother will die. I won't be able to pay the rent. It's the end. I'll never see the sun again. [*She breaks down in terrible sobs as Percy enters*]
Percy	Pretty grim, isn't it?

Rose Sorry?

Percy The night. Ghastly.

Rose The worst ever.

Percy Quite shocking.

Rose Yes. [*She breaks down into sobs again*]

Percy I say, it's not that bad! It might be sunny tomorrow.

Rose Can you help me find my flowers?

Percy I say, cheer up. Here's one down here. [*He puts it in her hand*] I say, your hand is jolly cold. And . . .

Rose Yes? What is it?

Percy Your face . . . it's so pale in the gas light.

Rose I'm very cold. [*She tries to smile*]

Percy And . . . such a pretty smile.

Rose Really?

Percy Truly.

Rose Truly?

Percy Really.

Rose And what is your face like? [*She puts out her hand and touches the lamp post*] You feel cold, yet so strong and smooth . . . with just a hint of rust.

Percy	You poor girl. [*He holds her hand*] You can't see, can you?
Rose	Not since the fire at the match factory.
Percy	Lord Septic's match factory?
Rose	Yes. I used to pack the match boxes. Big match boxes. Full of big matches.
Percy	Wasn't there a big strike at the match factory?
Rose	Yes. Lord Septic didn't pay us. He didn't keep the matches safe because it would cost him money. There was a fire and many workers were killed. I was lucky. But the flames hurt my eyes. I can't see any more.
Percy	What a rotter that man is! They've just gone on strike at another one of his factories. They all want a shorter working wick.
Rose	[*Laughing*] I think you mean WEEK. They want a shorter working WEEK.
Percy	No – it's a candle factory. I say, you look so pretty when you smile. What's your name?
Rose	My name is Rose.
Percy	A pure sweet rose! Then let me pick you and hold you under my nose! You need someone like me to look after you. Someone to take you home and put you in water.
Rose	Have you got a swimming pool?

15

Percy	No, but my front room has rising damp.
Rose	My attic room has dry rot. Our landlord is Lord Septic. He's so cruel to us.
[GULP]	
Percy	Poor Rose. If only I could give you some money. But all I have is my railway ticket. I was born with nothing. I'm an orphan. They say my mother was killed on this railway line.
[GASP]	
Rose	How very sad. You poor boy.
Percy	I was just a baby when they found me.
Rose	Where did they find you?
Percy	On this station – in the litter bin. I had nothing, apart from an apple core on my head and a little purse tied around my neck. There was no money in it, just a tiny key. It has a little sign with the letters NSL on it. I still wear it around my neck as a lucky charm. But I've had no luck so far. NSL must stand for No Such Luck.
Rose	Perhaps your luck will change tonight.
Percy	I think it already has. I've just met you!
Rose	Let me touch the key.
Percy	Of course. [*He takes her hand and puts it on his neck*] It's all I have from my past. I've never known what this key was for.

Rose	It could be the key to my heart! But I don't even know your name.
Percy	They called me 'purse key' at the workhouse. But it's just Percy now.
Rose	I wish I could help you.
Percy	And I wish I could help you, too. [*They are about to hug when Crouch storms on*]
[*HISS*]	
Crouch	Oi! You can cut that out for a start.
Rose	Oh no, it's him again. The man who threw away my flowers.
Percy	Did he, by jove?
Crouch	I told you to get lost.
Percy	Have you no shame, man? It's time I gave you a bit of your own treatment. How dare you harm a poor young girl. It's time to tell you what's what! [*He grabs Crouch by his collar*] It's time to show you how to treat a lady.
[*CHEER*]	
Crouch	[*Feebly*] I was only following orders, sir. It wasn't me. Don't blame me. Please.
Percy	Then pick up her flowers, you cad.
Crouch	Of course, sir. By all means, sir. Anything you say, sir.

Rose	Oh, Percy! You're my hero. My knight in shining armour. My good knight.
Crouch	Good knight?
Percy	Good knight!
Lord Septic	[*He creeps from the shadows and hits Percy on the head with his stick. Percy slumps to the ground.*] Good night!
[HISS]	
Crouch	Lord Septic!
Rose	Oh no. Lord Septic!
Lord Septic	THE Lord Septic.
[BOO]	
Rose	It's because of you I'm blind. It's because of you my mother is so ill in our slum. It's because of you I have nothing.
Lord Septic	Unlucky.
Rose	Until I tell my story. It's time I told the *Evening News* about your cruel ways.
Lord Septic	Grab her, Crouch. No one speaks to me like that. Tie her up. [*He grabs her by the wrist*]
[HISS]	
Crouch	Indeed, sir. Easy, sir. Of course, sir. Er . . . any idea where there's a rope?
Lord Septic	Down there by that trunk, you fool.

Crouch	Ah ha! And where shall I tie her, sir?
Lord Septic	Simple. Down there.
Crouch	Down there? You can't mean –
Lord Septic	Yes – tie her to the railway track. I can hear the midnight express.
[GASP]	
Rose	No, please! [*She faints*]
Percy	[*Dazed*] Let go of her.
Lord Septic	Just try and stop me! No one ever tells me what to do. It's time for you to take a closer look at the station lockers! [*He slams Percy against a locker, who falls down*] The only things I ever give away free are nose bleeds!
[BOO]	
Crouch	You're such a great man, Lord Septic.
Lord Septic	How true. Just look at these two feeble fools.
Crouch	That's two more 'F's, sir.
Lord Septic	They won't live to upset me again. I can snap them like twigs. I can crack them like nuts. I can pop them like pods.
Crouch	No one can snap, crackle and pop like you, sir.
Lord Septic	Just hurry and get her tied to the track. I can hear the train coming down the line.
Crouch	It just gave a chuff!

Lord Septic	Not as chuffed as I'll be when these two are pulp beneath its wheels. Ha! Dead chuffed! They'll be chuffed to bits!

[*Crouch ties Rose to the track. She stirs.*]

[*HISS, BOO*]

Crouch	Fear not, my dear. The roar of the midnight express will soon drown your screams. [*Percy staggers to his feet and runs off*] Look out – he's got away!
Lord Septic	Let him go. Who cares? He can't harm us. He's just a coward. He's running off up the track, into the path of the train!

[*GULP*]

Crouch	Then we'll kill two birds with one stone. Two fools with one express! I can feel the track shaking. It's not far away.
Lord Septic	She's such a pretty young thing. Your end is near, my dear.
Rose	Where am I? What's that noise?
Crouch	Just the sound of death!
Lord Septic	The Grim Reaper has a ticket on the midnight express! Ha ha.

[*GASP*]

Rose	Percy! Where is Percy? Percy!

Crouch	Too late. He's left you . . . and he's going under the wheels as we speak. Are you all right, sir? You've gone deathly still.
Lord Septic	It's just like that night many years ago. I stood right here as my father tied Lady Gatsby to the same track. She was the richest widow in town. He tricked her to meet him on this station one dark night.
Crouch	Killer trains must run in your family, sir!
Lord Septic	Lady Gatsby came here with her baby in one arm and the Gatsby Gold in the other. But somehow she hid it before we got our hands on it.
Crouch	You wanted to get the baby?
Lord Septic	No, the gold, you fool. It's worth a fortune. We tied her to this track to make her tell us where she'd hidden it.
Crouch	Did she tell?
Lord Septic	No. The train came early. We never found it. But it can't be far away. And I shall find it when I own the track and dig it up next week.
Rose	But what became of the poor baby?
Lord Septic	Bah! Who cares about the Gatsby Kid? I threw it away in the litter bin.
Rose	The litter bin? On this station?

Lord Septic	Yes, that one over there. He must have gone to the tip. The weedy brat never knew he was the heir to a fortune. It was years ago.
Crouch	A lot of trains have gone under the bridge since then, eh?
Rose	Percy! Oh Percy. It was Percy!
Lord Septic	[*He slaps her face*] Ah, shut your noise. Get ready to meet your doom!

[*HISS*]

Crouch	Here it comes . . . like thunder . . . like a dragon coming to slay the damsel.
Rose	The noise. The rails. The smoke.
Crouch	The sparks. The steam. The smell.
Lord Septic	The fog. The fear. The FUN!
Crouch	The END!

[*The rumble of the train grows louder. There is a sudden roar and a screech. There is smoke, sparks and a loud hiss. Percy leaps on with a chain, which he quickly winds round and round Crouch and Lord Septic. They fall in a heap. Percy cuts the rope, frees Rose and holds her in his arms.*]

[*CHEER*]

Percy	I'm back!
Rose	I'm shocked.
Crouch	I'm stuck.

Lord Septic	I'm livid.
Percy	You're safe.
Rose	You're here.
Percy	You're mine.
Rose	You're strong.
Percy	Your kiss . . .
Rose	Your lips . . .
Crouch	You're joking!
Rose	Percy, can it really be you?
Lord Septic	Untie this chain! Crouch, get your behind out of my face.
Crouch	I can't move, sir.
Rose	But . . . but . . . but how did you stop the train?
Percy	Do you really want to know?
Lord Septic	No one can stop the midnight express.
Percy	It wasn't easy. I had to take off my pants.
[*GASP*]	
Rose	How shocking!
Percy	The thing is . . . they're bright purple.
Crouch	How disgusting.
Lord Septic	How common.
Rose	How exciting!

Percy	And by the time I'd dabbed my nose bleed with my long-johns they were dark red.
Lord Septic	We don't want to know about your underwear.
Rose	I do!
Percy	I was just in time to climb up the gas lamp at the far end of the station. I put my pants over the lamp. It shone dark red. The train driver saw it in the nick of time.
Crouch	Don't you mean the KNICKERS of time?
[GROAN]	
Rose	Oh Percy! Your pants brought the train to a halt! They thought it was a stop light.
Lord Septic	Blast. You won't get away with this.
Percy	I told the guard on the train to call the police. They're on their way. You'll go to prison for this.
Crouch	No, please. I'll do anything . . .
Lord Septic	Shut up, you fool. Untie us at once. Someone pull this chain!
Percy	Oh no – you must never do that.
Rose	Why?
Percy	You must never pull the chain when the train is still in the station!
Rose	But there's something you need to know, Percy. SIR Percy!

Percy	Sir Percy?
Rose	Sir Percy Gatsby. The heir to the Gatsby Gold!
Lord Septic	Pah! You'll never find it.
Rose	The key! The key!
Percy	What key?
Crouch	Whose key?
Lord Septic	Which key?
Rose	Your key.
Percy	My key?
Rose	The key in the purse round your neck. The one your mother tied to you as a baby. The one with the sign NSL on it. That key must unlock the gold.
Crouch	NSL? That's the sign on the New Station Lockers. They were new many years ago.
Percy	Yes, of course! When I bashed my head into the locker over here, I saw the very same sign that's on my key. [*He runs to the locker and tries the key. It opens and he takes out a large heavy bag.*] I don't believe it! It's full of gold! I'm rich!
Lord Septic	Blast and double blast!
Rose	Oh Percy, your mother hid it there when you were a baby. I'm so happy for you.

Percy	No, Rose. Be happy for US. Half of this is yours. You can pay for the operation for you to see again. You can pay for your mother's pills to make her well again. You can pay for a new home. OUR home. I want you to marry me, Rose. All our fears are over. Will you be my wife?
Rose	Oh Percy! I love you!
Crouch	Yuk!
Lord Septic	This is the worst day of my life.
[CHEER]	
Percy	It's the last day of your life of crime. You'll soon be behind bars when we tell the world.
Crouch	You wouldn't.
Lord Septic	You couldn't.
Crouch	You shouldn't.
Lord Septic	You mustn't.
Crouch	You won't.
Lord Septic	You can't.
Crouch	You shan't.
Rose	We must.
Percy	We can.
Rose	We shall.

Percy	We will
Lord Septic	Who will?
Percy	I will.
Crouch	You will?
Rose	He will.
Lord Septic	He will?
Percy	She will.
Crouch	She will?
Rose/Percy	We both will!
Lord Septic	If you let us go, I'll pay. Name your price.
Percy	My price is JUSTICE!
[CHEER]	
Crouch	I can hear the police coming up the track.
Percy	Then it's time to hand you over. Come with me now, Rose. Let me take you away from here. Let's leave these villains to their fate. Walk this way . . .
Crouch	He has to walk that way – he hasn't got any pants on!
Percy	Our drama DRAWS to an end!
[GROAN]	
Rose	This morning I was nobody but you have made me a somebody. I'm so happy.

Percy	This morning I was nobody but you have made me a somebody. Now I have all I need.
Crouch	Apart from your pants! This morning I was nobody... nothing has changed.
Lord Septic	This morning I was somebody but you lot have made me a nobody. I'm sick to the back teeth of the lot of you. I'm really f...f...f...f...f...
Crouch	Fat? Foolish? Flabby? Feeble? Flea-infested?
Lord Septic	Shut your mouth, Crouch. Don't you think we've had enough 'F's for one night?
Rose	Even on such a foggy night our love is clear for all to see! And it all goes to show... Percy's purse and purple pants popped these plotters and their pranks!
Percy	And I've also popped the question. The question of my life. Will you marry me? Will you be mine forever? And... and...
Rose	Yes? What's your third question, Percy?
Percy	It's very chilly. Will you still love me if I go for some extra thick, heavy-duty, woolly, chunky, padded, thermal underwear?
Rose	Percy, I'll come with you. After all, from now on I will always love you through thick or thin!

[CHEER]

[*They freeze. They bow. The curtain falls.*]